Cross Stitch

Sweet Sentiments

2

8

12

Find the perfect sweet sentiment to stitch for yourself or a loved one!

5

17

Designs by Gail Bussi

LEISURE ARTS, INC. • Maumelle, Arkansas

Plant a garden
trusting in the
Lord's promise

Noah's Garden

Only after rainy days will a garden grow to its full potential. Remember the promise of sunnier days ahead with this uplifting design.

Stitch Count = 41w × 101h

FABRIC SIZE

- One 9" × 13" (22.9cm × 33.0cm) piece of 28-ct. Star Sapphire Jobelan® by Wichelt Imports (stitched over two threads)

DESIGN SIZE

- 25-ct. = 3¼" × 8⅛" (8.3cm × 20.6cm)
- 28-ct. = 2⅞" × 7¼" (7.3cm × 18.4cm)
- 32-ct. = 2½" × 6⅜" (6.4cm × 16.2cm)

EMBELLISHMENTS

- One small pewter bee charm
- One small pewter butterfly charm

INSTRUCTIONS

Center the design and begin stitching over two fabric threads. Use either two strands of cotton embroidery floss, Gentle Art Simply Shaker™ thread, or Gentle Art Sampler™ thread, or one strand of #12 pearl cotton to work cross stitches. To maximize color changes when stitching with Gentle Art thread, complete each cross stitch before moving on to the next one. Work three-sided stitches with one strand of #12 pearl cotton. Use one strand of #12 pearl cotton or Gentle Art Sampler thread to work satin stitches. Work French knots with one strand of cotton embroidery floss. Use one strand of cotton embroidery floss or Gentle Art Simply Shaker thread to work backstitches. Use one strand of cotton embroidery floss to attach butterfly and bee charms where indicated. Place the needlework facedown on a terry cloth towel and carefully press the needlework from the back before framing as desired.

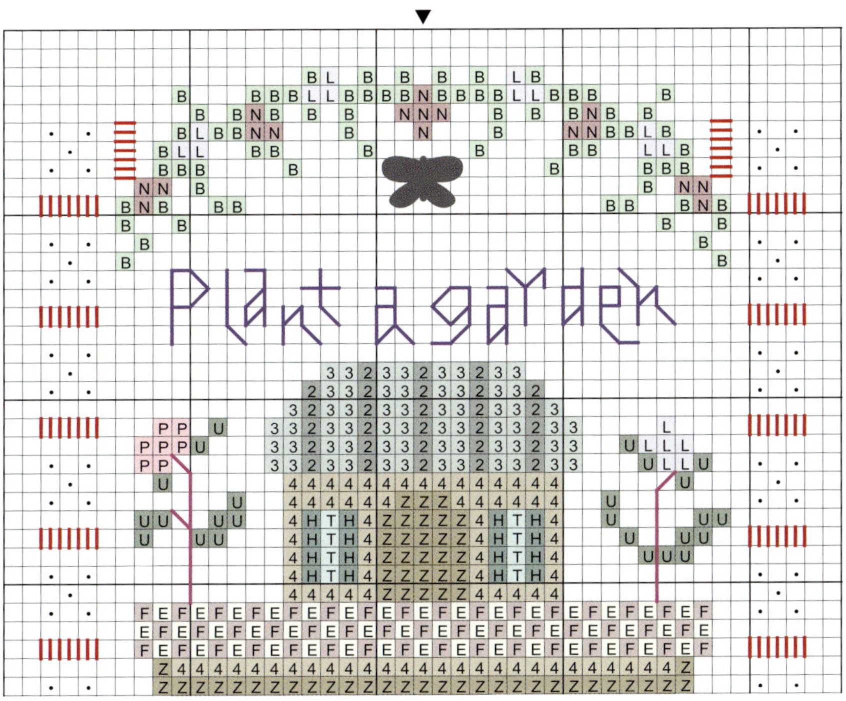

Specialty Stitches

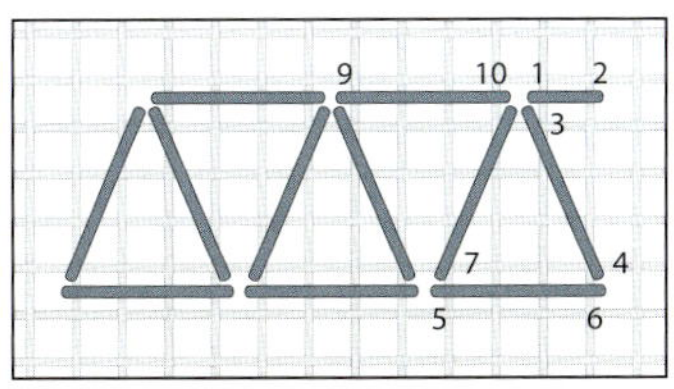

Three-Sided Stitch

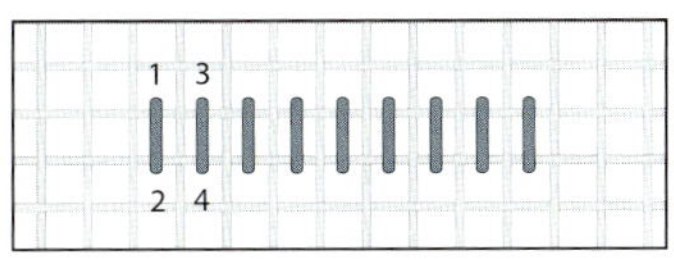

Satin Stitch

Color key can be found on page 4.

CROSS STITCH

ANCHOR		DMC	COLOR
895	F	223	Light Shell Pink
860	V	522	Fern Green
392	C	642	Dark Beige Gray
830	5	644	Medium Beige Gray
8581	2	646	Dark Beaver Gray
900	3	648	Light Beaver Gray
379	Z	840	Medium Beige Brown
850	H	926	Medium Gray Green
848	J	927	Light Gray Green
274	T	928	Very Light Gray Green
888	6	3045	Dark Yellow Beige
887	Y	3046	Medium Yellow Beige
393	S	3790	Ultra Dark Beige Gray
376	4	3864	Light Mocha Beige

ANCHOR #12 PEARL COTTON		DMC #12 PEARL COTTON	COLOR
002	•	White	White

GENTLE ART SAMPLER		COLOR
0130	W	Avocado
0150	B	Evergreen
0820	L	Lavender Potpourri
0830	N	Highland Heather

GENTLE ART SIMPLY SHAKER		COLOR
7003	U	Shutter Green
7014	P	Antique Rose
7025	E	Shaker White

FRENCH KNOT

ANCHOR		DMC	COLOR
871	•	3041	Medium Antique Violet

BACKSTITCH

ANCHOR		DMC	COLOR
871	—	3041	Medium Antique Violet
393	—	3790	Ultra Dark Beige Gray

GENTLE ART SIMPLY SHAKER		COLOR
7003	—	Shutter Green

SATIN STITCH

ANCHOR #12 PEARL COTTON		DMC #12 PEARL COTTON	COLOR
002	IIIII	White	White

GENTLE ART SAMPLER		COLOR
0820	IIIII	Lavender Potpourri

THREE-SIDED STITCH

ANCHOR #12 PEARL COTTON		DMC #12 PEARL COTTON	COLOR
002	▽	White	White

Bright blue area indicates last row of previous section of design.

Project Tip

Stitching with Over-Dyed Floss
When stitching with over-dyed floss such as Gentle Art threads, complete each cross stitch in full before moving on to the next. This method will keep the gradual color changes of the floss in your stitching. The traditional method of completing an entire row of half cross stitches before going back and finishing the full cross stitches will result in a more uniform color because the subtle variations will be lost.

A Song of Thanks

A little bird tweets out a thankful song in this sweet design. The autumnal colors and motifs will be right at home with your fall and Thanksgiving décor.

Fill your heart...with a song of thanks

Stitch Count = 96w × 96h

FABRIC

- One 15" × 15" (38.1cm × 38.1cm) piece of 28-ct. French Vanilla Swirl Over-Dyed Cashel® Linen by Zweigart® (stitched over two threads)

DESIGN SIZE

- 25-ct. = 7⁵/₈" × 7⁵/₈" (19.4cm × 19.4cm)
- 28-ct. = 6⁷/₈" × 6⁷/₈" (17.5cm × 17.5cm)
- 32-ct. = 6" × 6" (15.2cm × 15.2cm)

INSTRUCTIONS

Center the design and begin stitching over two fabric threads. Work cross stitches and quarter cross stitches with two strands of cotton embroidery floss. Use two strands of DMC® 355/Anchor 1014 to work the backstitches and French knots of the lettering. Work all other backstitches and French knots with one strand of cotton embroidery floss. Use a pressing cloth to carefully iron the needlework from the back before framing as desired.

CROSS STITCH

ANCHOR		DMC	COLOR
1047	I	402	Very Light Mahogany
858	E	524	Very Light Fern Green
933	S	543	Ultra Very Light Beige Brown
891	B	676	Light Old Gold
300	O	745	Light Pale Yellow
1002	N	977	Light Golden Brown
266	L	3347	Medium Yellow Green
264	K	3348	Light Yellow Green
262	C	3363	Medium Pine Green
260	D	3364	Pine Green
1048	H	3776	Light Mahogany
868	P	3779	Ultra Very Light Terra Cotta
1050	F	3781	Dark Mocha Brown
365	M	3826	Golden Brown
373	A	3828	Hazelnut Brown
1010	J	3856	Ultra Very Light Mahogany
379	T	3863	Medium Mocha Beige
376	R	3864	Light Mocha Beige
002	•	3865	Winter White

FRENCH KNOT

ANCHOR		DMC	COLOR
1014	•	355	Dark Terra Cotta
1002	•	977	Light Golden Brown
002	•	3865	Winter White

BACKSTITCH

ANCHOR		DMC	COLOR
1014	—	355	Dark Terra Cotta
1002	—	977	Light Golden Brown
262	—	3363	Medium Pine Green
1050	—	3781	Dark Mocha Brown

Bright blue area indicates last row of previous section of design.

Bee Blessed

Even when life has us buzzing from one thing to another like busy little bees, this sweet design reminds us to slow down and be thankful for the joys in our lives.

Stitch Count = 114w × 100h

FABRIC SIZE

- One 16" × 16" (40.6cm × 40.6cm) piece of 28-ct. Mushroom Jazlyn® by Wichelt Imports (stitched over two threads)

DESIGN SIZE

- 25-ct. = 9 1/8" × 8" (23.2cm × 20.3cm)
- 28-ct. = 8 1/8" × 7 1/8" (20.6cm × 18.1cm)
- 32-ct. = 7 1/8" × 6 1/4" (18.1cm × 15.9cm)

INSTRUCTIONS

Center the design and begin stitching over two fabric threads. Work cross stitches, half cross stitches, and quarter cross stitches with two strands of cotton embroidery floss or two strands of Gentle Art Simply Shaker™ thread. To maximize color changes when stitching with Simply Shaker thread, complete each cross stitch before moving on to the next one. Work backstitches and French knots with one strand of cotton embroidery floss or one strand of Simply Shaker thread. Use a pressing cloth to carefully iron the needlework from the back before framing as desired.

Color key can be found on page 11.

Bee Blessed A

Bee Blessed B

Bee Blessed C

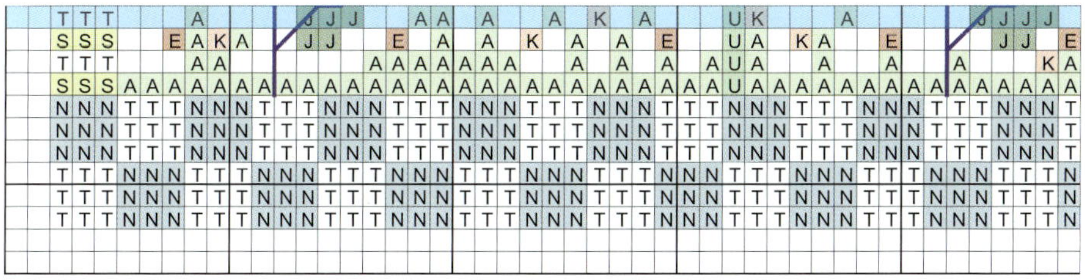

Bee Blessed D

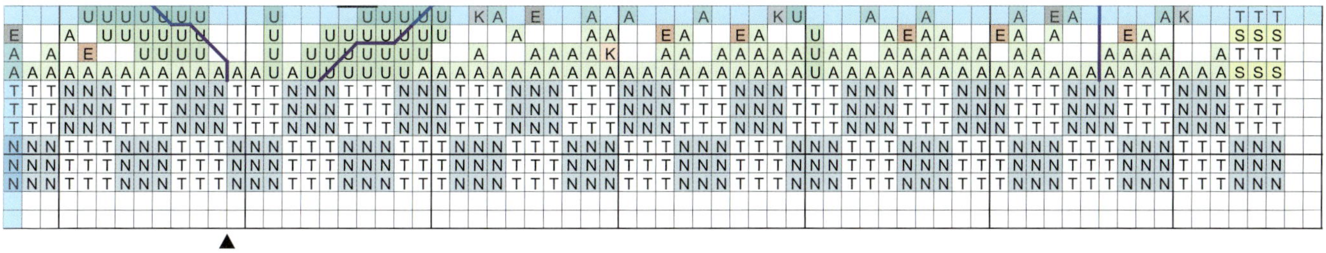

CROSS STITCH

ANCHOR		DMC	COLOR
5975	E	356	Light Medium Terra Cotta
858	A	524	Very Light Fern Green
301	B	744	Pale Yellow
882	K	758	Very Light Terra Cotta
234	C	762	Very Light Pearl Gray
887	F	3046	Medium Yellow Beige
852	D	3047	Light Yellow Beige
260	J	3364	Pine Green
1050	R	3781	Dark Mocha Brown
358	G	3862	Dark Mocha Beige
002	T	3865	Winter White

GENTLE ART SIMPLY SHAKER		COLOR
7003	U	Shutter Green
7006	N	Old Blue Paint
7020	S	Butternut Squash

FRENCH KNOT

ANCHOR		DMC	COLOR
262	•	3363	Medium Pine Green
1050	•	3781	Dark Mocha Brown

GENTLE ART SIMPLY SHAKER		COLOR
7020	•	Butternut Squash

BACKSTITCH

ANCHOR		DMC	COLOR
5975	—	356	Light Medium Terra Cotta
262	—	3363	Medium Pine Green
1050	—	3781	Dark Mocha Brown
002	—	3865	Winter White

GENTLE ART SIMPLY SHAKER		COLOR
7020	—	Butternut Squash

Bright blue area indicates last row of previous section of design.

Project Tip

Prevent Twisting
During the movement of stitching, the needle naturally twists, which can cause loops and knots in the thread. To prevent this, work several stitches, then make note of which way the thread unwinds when you hang it straight down from your work. Give your needle a partial turn in that direction with each stitch to keep the thread from twisting.

Bee Blessed Chart Diagram

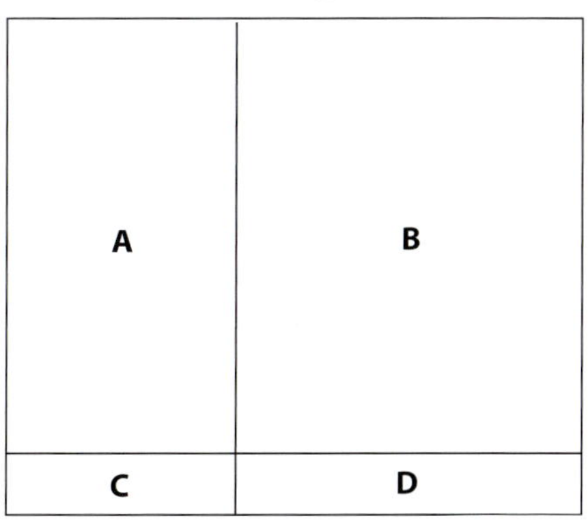

Count Your Blessings

Sunny days, tea in the garden, friends, and family:

This cheerful design highlights some of the wonderful things in our lives that make us truly blessed.

Stitch Count = 140w × 113h

FABRIC SIZE

- One 17" × 15" (43.2cm × 38.1cm) piece of 32-ct. Antique White Jobelan® by Wichelt Imports (stitched over two threads)

DESIGN SIZE

- 25-ct. = 11¼" × 9" (28.6cm × 22.9cm)
- 28-ct. = 10" × 8" (25.4cm × 20.3cm)
- 32-ct. = 8¾" × 7" (22.2cm × 17.8cm)

INSTRUCTIONS

Center the design and begin stitching over two fabric threads. Work cross stitches, quarter cross stitches, and half cross stitches with two strands of cotton embroidery floss. Work French knots and backstitches with one strand of cotton embroidery floss. Use a pressing cloth to carefully iron the needlework from the back before framing as desired.

Color key can be found on page 15.

Count Your Blessings A

Count Your Blessings B

Count Your Blessings C

CROSS STITCH

ANCHOR		DMC	COLOR
002	•	White	White
399	F	318	Light Steel Gray
215	K	320	Medium Pistachio Green
214	O	368	Light Pistachio Green
310	N	434	Light Brown
1045	A	436	Tan
877	B	502	Blue Green
858	7	524	Very Light Fern Green
098	J	553	Violet
096	8	554	Light Violet
057	W	601	Dark Cranberry
062	U	603	Cranberry
830	C	644	Medium Beige Gray
300	2	745	Light Pale Yellow
1012	S	754	Light Peach
390	Q	822	Light Beige Gray
1034	G	931	Medium Antique Blue
1033	P	932	Light Antique Blue
073	R	963	Ultra Very Light Dusty Rose
262	E	3363	Medium Pine Green
260	H	3364	Pine Green
1032	T	3752	Very Light Antique Blue
393	D	3790	Ultra Dark Beige Gray
386	L	3823	Ultra Pale Yellow
311	Y	3855	Light Autumn Gold
002	Z	3865	Winter White

FRENCH KNOT

ANCHOR		DMC	COLOR
057	•	601	Dark Cranberry
1035	•	930	Dark Antique Blue
393	•	3790	Ultra Dark Beige Gray
311	•	3855	Light Autumn Gold

BACKSTITCH

ANCHOR	DMC	COLOR
057	601	Dark Cranberry
1035	930	Dark Antique Blue
262	3363	Medium Pine Green
393	3790	Ultra Dark Beige Gray
311	3855	Light Autumn Gold

Bright blue area indicates last row of previous section of design.

Count Your Blessings D

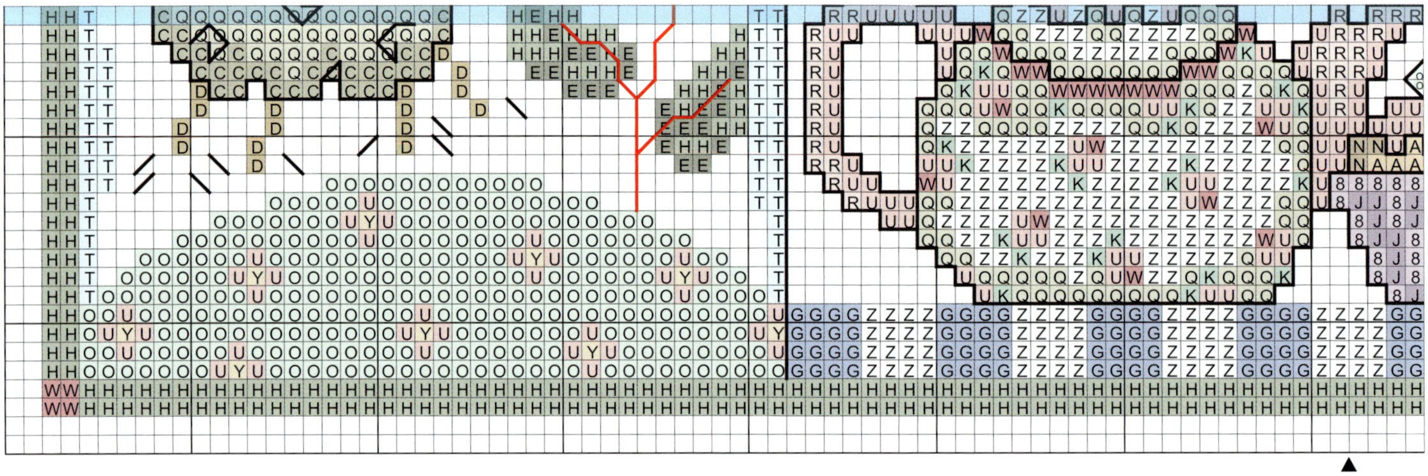

Count Your Blessings E

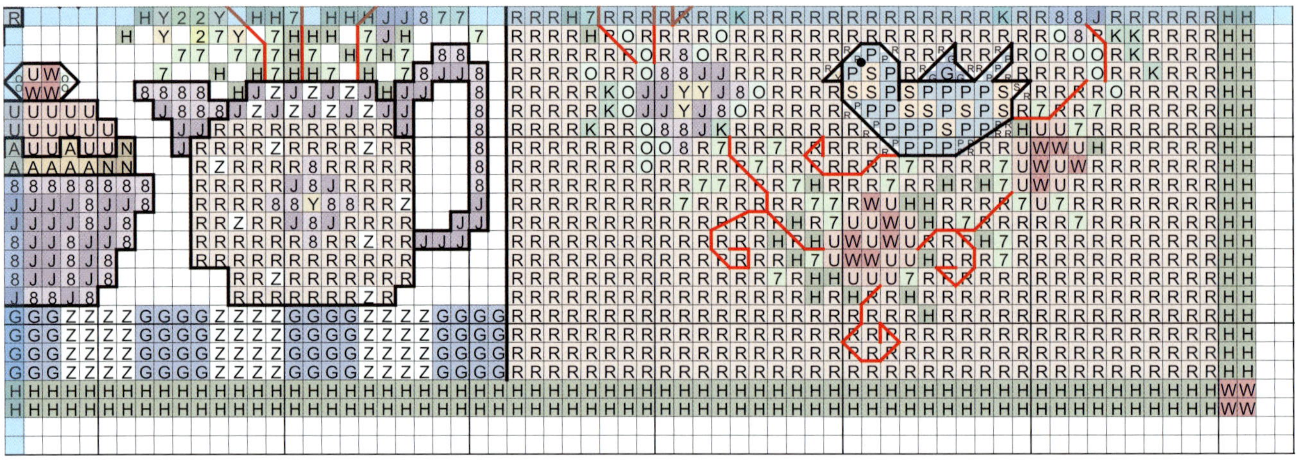

Count Your Blessings Chart Diagram

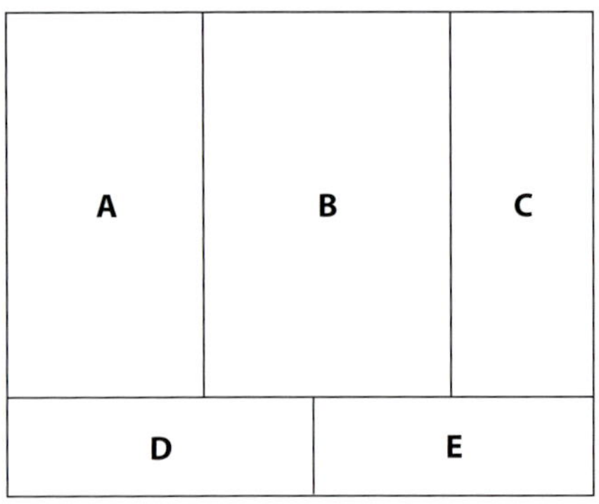

Bright blue area indicates last row of previous section of design.

CROSS STITCH

ANCHOR		DMC	COLOR
002	•	White	White
399	F	318	Light Steel Gray
215	K	320	Medium Pistachio Green
214	O	368	Light Pistachio Green
310	N	434	Light Brown
1045	A	436	Tan
877	B	502	Blue Green
858	7	524	Very Light Fern Green
098	J	553	Violet
096	8	554	Light Violet
057	W	601	Dark Cranberry
062	U	603	Cranberry
830	C	644	Medium Beige Gray
300	2	745	Light Pale Yellow
1012	S	754	Light Peach
390	Q	822	Light Beige Gray
1034	G	931	Medium Antique Blue
1033	P	932	Light Antique Blue
073	R	963	Ultra Very Light Dusty Rose
262	E	3363	Medium Pine Green

CROSS STITCH

ANCHOR		DMC	COLOR
260	H	3364	Pine Green
1032	T	3752	Very Light Antique Blue
393	D	3790	Ultra Dark Beige Gray
386	L	3823	Ultra Pale Yellow
311	Y	3855	Light Autumn Gold
002	Z	3865	Winter White

FRENCH KNOT

ANCHOR		DMC	COLOR
057	•	601	Dark Cranberry
1035	•	930	Dark Antique Blue
393	•	3790	Ultra Dark Beige Gray
311	•	3855	Light Autumn Gold

BACKSTITCH

ANCHOR		DMC	COLOR
057	—	601	Dark Cranberry
1035	—	930	Dark Antique Blue
262	—	3363	Medium Pine Green
393	—	3790	Ultra Dark Beige Gray
311	—	3855	Light Autumn Gold

Bluebird Celebration

With its soft color palette and delightful floral border, this charming design is the perfect way to celebrate a wedding.

Bluebird Celebration A

Bluebird Celebration B

Stitch Count = 125w × 125h

FABRIC SIZE

- One 17" × 17" (43.2cm × 43.2cm) piece of 28-ct. Summer Sky Hand-Dyed Jobelan® by Wichelt Imports (stitched over two threads)

DESIGN SIZE

- 25-ct. = 10" × 10" (25.4cm × 25.4cm)
- 28-ct. = $8\frac{7}{8}$" × $8\frac{7}{8}$" (22.5cm × 22.5cm)
- 32-ct. = $7\frac{3}{4}$" × $7\frac{3}{4}$" (19.7cm × 19.7cm)

(continued on page 20)

CROSS STITCH

ANCHOR	Symbol	DMC	COLOR
240	J	164	Light Forest Green
109	F	209	Dark Lavender
399	Z	318	Light Steel Gray
374	P	420	Dark Hazelnut Brown
943	R	422	Light Hazelnut Brown
858	L	524	Very Light Fern Green
096	E	554	Light Violet
830	2	644	Medium Beige Gray
301	Q	744	Pale Yellow
1012	S	754	Light Peach
390	W	822	Light Beige Gray
379	V	840	Medium Beige Brown
378	U	841	Light Beige Brown
388	T	842	Very Light Beige Brown
1034	I	931	Medium Antique Blue
1033	Y	932	Light Antique Blue
073	A	963	Ultra Very Light Dusty Rose
243	K	988	Medium Forest Green
074	B	3354	Light Dusty Rose
260	M	3364	Pine Green
076	D	3731	Very Dark Dusty Rose
075	C	3733	Dusty Rose
1032	G	3752	Very Light Antique Blue
002	O	3865	Winter White

FRENCH KNOT

ANCHOR	Symbol	DMC	COLOR
301	• (yellow)	744	Pale Yellow
273	• (black)	3787	Dark Brown Gray

BACKSTITCH

ANCHOR	Symbol	DMC	COLOR
109	—	209	Dark Lavender
379	—	840	Medium Beige Brown
1034	—	931	Medium Antique Blue
262	—	3363	Medium Pine Green
076	—	3731	Very Dark Dusty Rose
273	—	3787	Dark Brown Gray

Bright blue area indicates last row of previous section of design.

Bluebird Celebration C

(continued from page 19)

INSTRUCTIONS

Center the design and begin stitching over two fabric threads. Use the accompanying alphabet chart to personalize the design. Work cross stitches, half cross stitches, and quarter cross stitches with two strands of cotton embroidery floss. Work letter backstitches with two strands of DMC® 3731/Anchor 076 or DMC 3787/Anchor 273; work all other backstitches with one strand of cotton embroidery floss. Work DMC 3787/Anchor 273 French knots with two strands of cotton embroidery floss; work all other French knots with one strand of cotton embroidery floss. Use a pressing cloth to carefully iron the needlework from the back before framing as desired.

Bluebird Celebration Chart Diagram

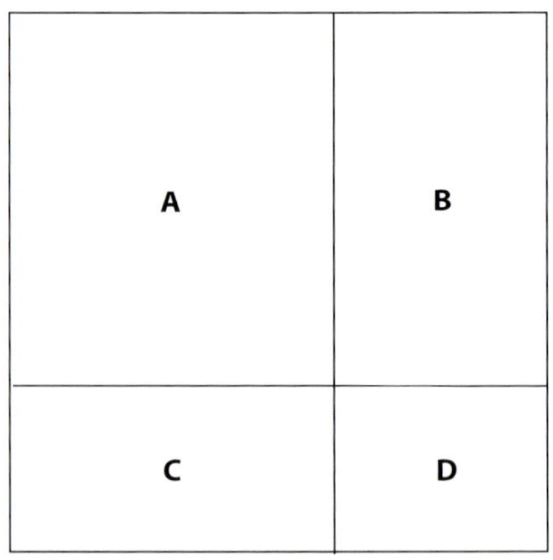

Project Tip

Keeping Fabric Clean in a Hoop

When using a hoop, try putting a sheet of white tissue paper in the hoop on top of the fabric. Tear away the tissue paper in the area where you are stitching. This keeps oils from your hands from getting on the fabric and helps keep the needlework piece free from stains. And whether you use a hoop or not, always wash and dry your hands completely before starting any stitching.

Bluebird Celebration D

CROSS STITCH

ANCHOR		DMC	COLOR
240	J	164	Light Forest Green
109	F	209	Dark Lavender
399	Z	318	Light Steel Gray
374	P	420	Dark Hazelnut Brown
943	R	422	Light Hazelnut Brown
858	L	524	Very Light Fern Green
096	E	554	Light Violet
830	2	644	Medium Beige Gray
301	Q	744	Pale Yellow
1012	S	754	Light Peach
390	W	822	Light Beige Gray
379	V	840	Medium Beige Brown
378	U	841	Light Beige Brown
388	T	842	Very Light Beige Brown
1034	I	931	Medium Antique Blue
1033	Y	932	Light Antique Blue
073	A	963	Ultra Very Light Dusty Rose
243	K	988	Medium Forest Green
074	B	3354	Light Dusty Rose

CROSS STITCH

ANCHOR		DMC	COLOR
260	M	3364	Pine Green
076	D	3731	Very Dark Dusty Rose
075	C	3733	Dusty Rose
1032	G	3752	Very Light Antique Blue
002	O	3865	Winter White

FRENCH KNOT

ANCHOR		DMC	COLOR
301	•	744	Pale Yellow
273	•	3787	Dark Brown Gray

BACKSTITCH

ANCHOR		DMC	COLOR
109	—	209	Dark Lavender
379	—	840	Medium Beige Brown
1034	—	931	Medium Antique Blue
262	—	3363	Medium Pine Green
076	—	3731	Very Dark Dusty Rose
273	—	3787	Dark Brown Gray

Bright blue area indicates last row of previous section of design.

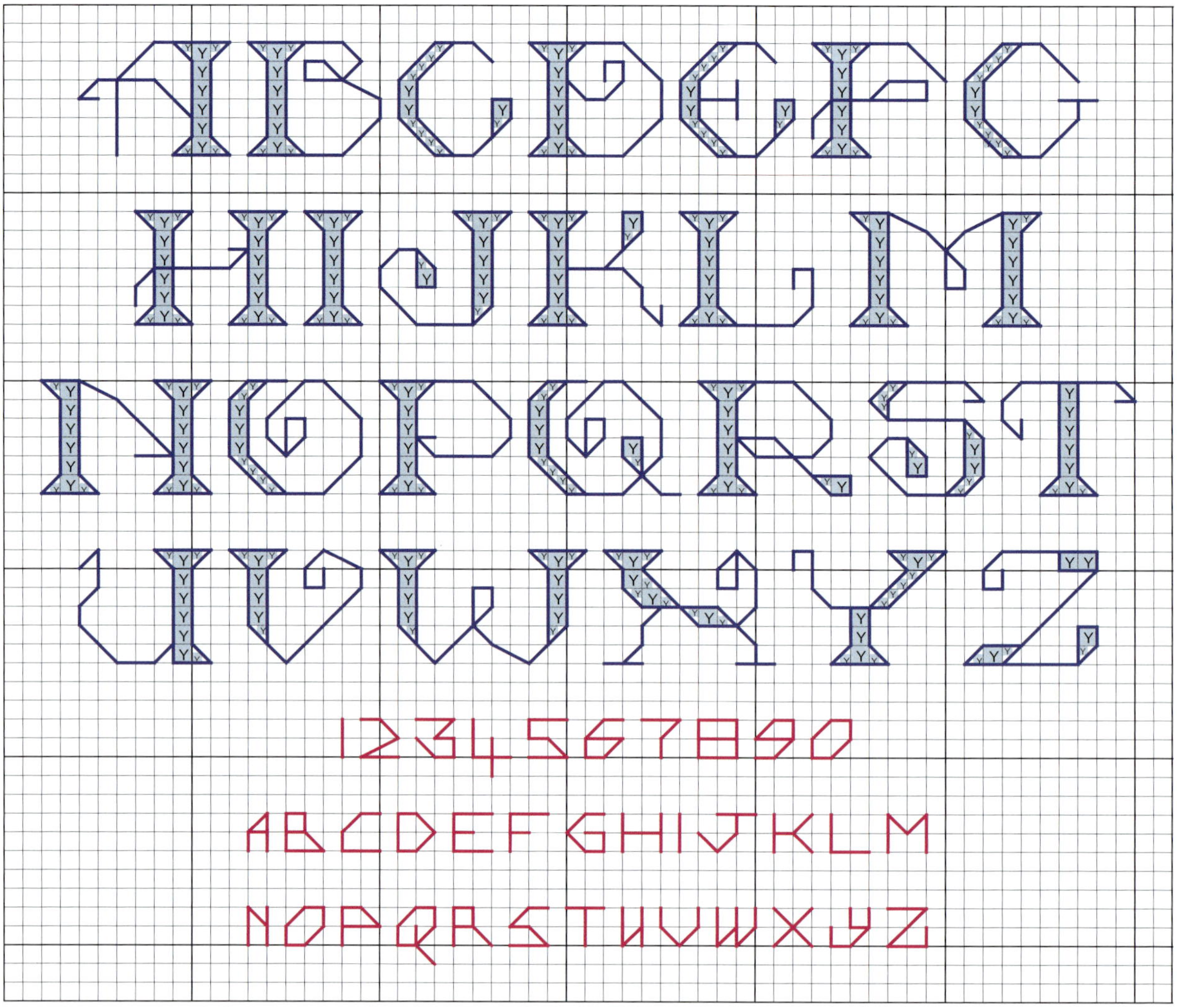

CROSS STITCH

ANCHOR		DMC	COLOR
1033	Y	932	Light Antique Blue

BACKSTITCH

ANCHOR		DMC	COLOR
1034	——	931	Medium Antique Blue
076	——	3731	Very Dark Dusty Rose

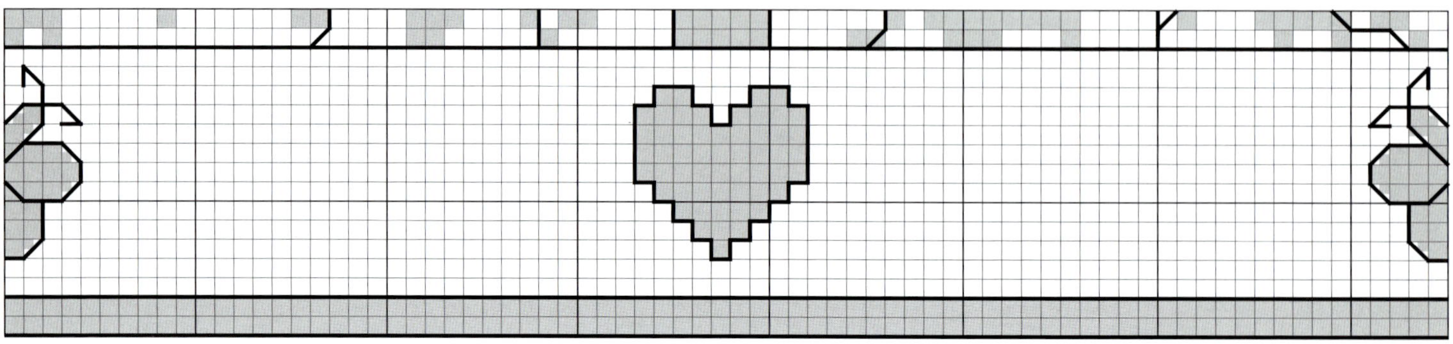

Project Tip

Personalizing Your Design

Use the accompanying alphabet and the grid on the opposite page to personalize Bluebird Celebration. The gray areas on the grid indicate the stitched areas in the main design, and the empty area indicates the space you have to work with to personalize the design. Refer to the instructions below for how to chart the initials and wedding date within this grid, then stitch according to the stitching instructions on page 20.

You can also use the alphabet to stitch a name, monogram, or date on another design. To personalize a piece of fabric or a larger design, begin by counting the stitchable area you have to work with (stitches wide by stitches high). Mark this area on the blank grid above. Find the center of the stitchable area and the center of the name or monogram—this will determine if a letter or a space will be at the center.

Begin charting the name or monogram onto the blank grid, centering the middle letter or space and working outward. Use a pencil for this, as you may need to adjust the spacing so as to best utilize the area. In most cases, one or two empty rows between letters will work best, but some thin letters (I, L, T, etc.) may look better with more empty rows around them. Be consistent, and make sure the name or monogram looks even and balanced.

Match up the center of the fabric to the center of your graphed letters. Begin stitching at the center and work out to be sure the lettering is centered correctly on the fabric.

General Instructions

Getting Started

For most projects, the starting point is at the center. Every chart has arrows that indicate the horizontal and vertical centers. With your finger, trace along the grid to the point where the two centers meet. Compare a symbol at the center of the chart to the key and choose which floss color to stitch first. To find the center of the fabric, fold it into quarters and finger-crease.

Cut the floss into 15" lengths and separate all six strands. Recombine the appropriate number of strands and thread them into a blunt-tip needle. Refer to each project's instructions for number of floss strands to use for stitches.

To Secure Thread at the Beginning

The most common way to secure the beginning tail of the thread is to hold it on the wrong side of the fabric under the first four or five stitches.

To Secure Thread at the End

To finish, slip the threaded needle under previously stitched threads on the wrong side of the fabric for four or five stitches, weaving the thread back and forth a few times. Clip the thread.

Framing Your Pieces

Iron the finished needlework on the wrong side using a dry pressing cloth and medium temperature setting; do not steam. Accurately measure the length and width of your completed piece before purchasing a mat or frame. Consulting a professional framer or art supply store to mat and frame your design is recommended.

Cross Stitch

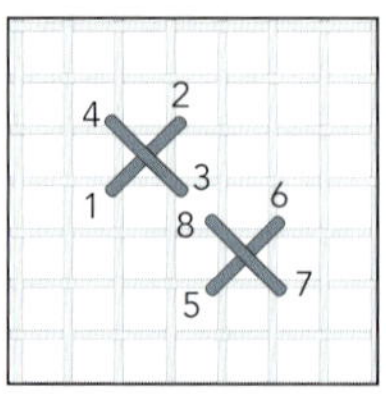

Make one cross stitch for each symbol on the chart. For horizontal rows, stitch the first diagonal of each stitch in the row. Work back across the row, completing each stitch. On most linen and evenweave fabrics, work the stitches over two threads as shown in the diagram. For aida cloth, each stitch fills one square. You also can work cross stitches in the reverse direction. Remember to embroider the stitches uniformly—that is, always work the top half of each stitch in the same direction.

Quarter and Three-Quarter Cross Stitches

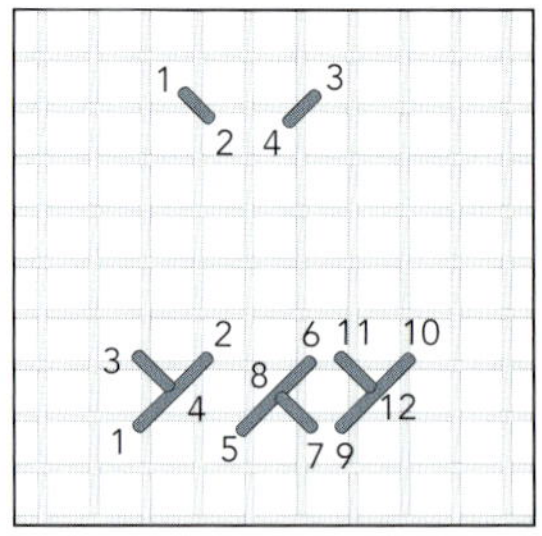

To obtain rounded shapes in a design, use quarter and three-quarter cross stitches. On linen and evenweave fabrics, a quarter stitch will extend from the corner to the center intersection of the threads. To make quarter cross stitches on aida cloth, estimate the center of the square. Three-quarter cross stitches combine a quarter cross stitch with a half cross stitch. Both stitches may slant in any direction.

Half Cross Stitches

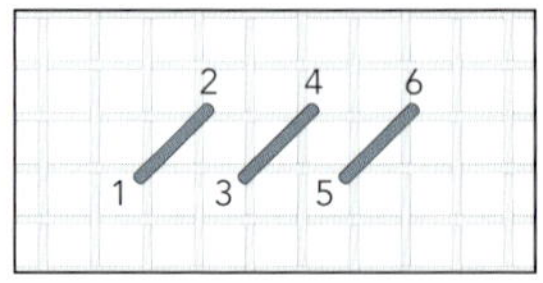

A half cross stitch is a single diagonal or half a cross stitch. They are indicated on the chart by a diagonal colored symbol.

Backstitches

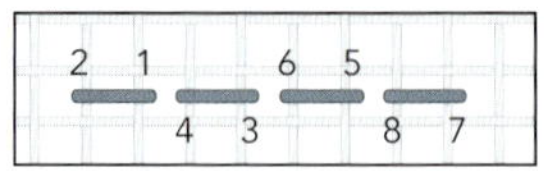

Working from right to left, bring the needle up from the back side of the fabric, one stitch length from your starting point. Begin the next stitch by inserting the needle at your starting point and back up two stitch lengths away. Continue, keeping all the stitches the same length.

French Knot

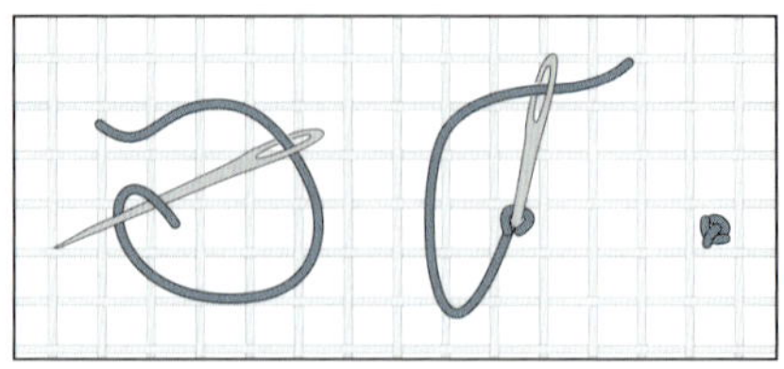

Bring the threaded needle through the fabric and wrap the floss around the needle as shown. Tighten the twists and return the needle through the fabric in the same place. The floss will slide through the wrapped thread to make the knot.

Produced by Herrschners, Inc., for distribution exclusively by Leisure Arts, Inc., 104 Champs Blvd., STE 100, Maumelle, AR 72113-6738, leisurearts.com.